SALLY ANNA is Curious

ISBN: 978-1-63813-225-7

Cover and text layout design: Kristi Yoder

Printed in China

Published by:

TGS International
P.O. Box 355
Berlin, Ohio 44610 USA
Phone: 330.893.4828
Fax: 330.893.4893
www.tgsinternational.com

SALLY ANNA is Curious

Written and illustrated by Eva Zimmerman

Introduction

Sally Anna, the curious goat who sticks her nose into all the goings on around her, was real.

So was Mamma Cat, who caught snakes in the creek and carried them, wriggling and squirming, to the barn to feed her kittens.

A goat wandering too close to the beehives, the new puppy's broken leg, and the flood with the animals on a hillock are all true incidents.

Sally Anna's story is based on these true happenings.

—Eva Zimmerman

Sally Anna was a frisky little goat. She lived in the barn with Little Pony. Sally Anna was a curious goat. To her the whole wide world was just waiting to be explored. She was always sticking her little goat nose into this thing and that thing to see what she could find.

One day Little Pony was led out of the barn. Sally Anna was curious. Where was Little Pony going? Out the door she slipped with Little Pony. Now Sally Anna was free! She forgot all about Little Pony as she skipped and danced and pranced about, finding new and wonderful things. Light as a feather, skipping here and there, she stayed just out of reach. With a bounce and a flounce, now sideways, now forward, now up, now down Sally Anna went. What fun! What fun! Then, with one more dance and one more prance, Sally Anna was chased back into the barn.

From the barn door Sally Anna could see the whole wide green meadow that was hers to play in. Into the green meadow Sally Anna went to see what there was to see. And she saw something. Oh yes, she did!

Across the green meadow from the big creek came Mamma Cat with her head held high. Sally Anna was curious. What was Mamma Cat doing? With a skip and a hop, she raced off to meet Mamma Cat.

Now Mamma Cat was a hunter. She hunted mice, but that was not the only thing she hunted. She hunted snakes! In her mouth she carried a wriggly, squiggly snake! She had caught it in the creek and was on her way to the barn to feed her hungry kittens. The snake wriggled and squirmed. Sally Anna bounced and scampered all about. Mamma Cat just kept marching on toward the barn.

So away Sally Anna trotted in search of something new.

Through the green meadow Sally Anna wandered, tasting anything and everything. A clump of pretty flowers grew in the tall grass. "Sniff, sniff!" went Sally Anna's little goat nose. How good they smelled! "Nibble, nibble!" went her little goat mouth. How good they tasted!

The honeybees were at the flowers too. Sally Anna was curious. What were they doing? She raced after the bees.

Nearby stood a row of beehives. This is where the honeybees lived. The bees were busy. Back and forth flew many busy bees, back and forth making honey. Sally Anna stuck her nose up to the beehives. "Sniff, sniff!" she went.

"Buzz! Buzz! Buzz!" went the bees. They did not like a goat at their beehive home. "Sting! Sting! Sting!" went many angry bees on Sally Anna's nose and belly. They even stung her little goat tail. How Sally Anna kicked and bucked and ran! How she cried! The bees chased her, stinging and stinging and stinging. Poor Sally Anna!

Someone heard Sally Anna's cries. Cool water soothed her hot skin. Medicine helped her feel better. Sally Anna had learned a lesson, and she had learned it the hard way. Never again did she go near the beehives.

Soon Sally Anna was feeling much better. *Skip! Prance! Leap!* She kicked up her heels and off she went to see what she could find. And she found it. Oh yes, she did!

At the green meadows lived a new puppy named Jethro. How that puppy and Sally Anna played! Jethro used his sharp little puppy teeth to nip at Sally Anna. Sally Anna used her sharp little goat horns to butt Jethro. Such a running and leaping and rolling those two had!

Jethro was just a pup. He had not learned the rule about staying off the road. After their playing, Jethro ran out on the road. He ran after a bicycle. The louder he barked, the faster the bicycle went. What fun! What fun!

Sally Anna was eating grass inside her meadow. She saw a car coming and saw it hit Jethro. She heard Jethro's cries and saw him going away in another car.

When Jethro came home, a shiny new cast was on his front leg.

Sally Anna was curious. What had happened to her new friend? She sniffed at the cast. Jethro whimpered. He was not playing and jumping now. Oh no, he wasn't! He had learned a lesson the hard way, just like Sally Anna had.

In a few weeks Jethro was feeling better. A cast did not keep sharp little puppy teeth from nipping. It did not keep sharp little goat horns away. *Roll! Leap! Frolic!* went Sally Anna and Jethro at their play!

Then something new came to Sally Anna's little world. A hurricane blew in. It rained and rained and rained. The little creek grew bigger and bigger until it was a rushing river. Higher and higher came the water until the little creek and the big creek were one big flood.

Sally Anna was safe and dry in her barn. But when the rain stopped, she wasted no time in going outside to see what there was to see. She saw water everywhere! She was curious. What had happened to her green meadow? Closer and closer to the water she went.

Not far away were some cows that had got caught in the rainstorm. Away Sally Anna ran, as fast as the wind, to see what those cows were doing.

But the rain was not over yet. It rained hard and fast again. The water rose higher and higher until Sally Anna and the cows were trapped.

The cows were wet and hungry. They had been out in the storm long enough. With a splash they waded into the deep water and headed for the barn.

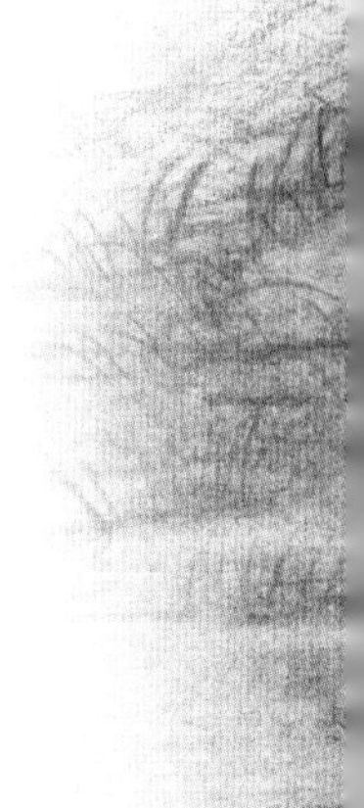

But Sally Anna's legs were short. They were meant for skipping and jumping. They were not meant for wading through deep water. She could not follow the cows. She was left all alone on the little green island. She was cold, she was wet, and she was scared.

Someone saw the trouble Sally Anna was in. Someone came and carried her to the barn. Sally Anna snuggled down in the warm dry straw. She had had enough excitement for one day!

But she did not stop being curious. There were so many things that made Sally Anna happy—the grass, the flowers, the trees, the animals—Sally Anna liked them all.

Day after happy day she found so many things to enjoy.

How great is the world we live in.
How good is our God who made it all!

All things bright and beautiful
All creatures great and small;
All things wise and wonderful,
The Lord God made them all.

"Thou hast created all things,
and for thy pleasure they are
and were created."
Revelation 4:11b

"God . . . giveth us richly all things to enjoy."
1 Timothy 6:17

THE END

About the Author

Eva Zimmerman lives in Lancaster County, Pennsylvania, where she taught special education for 25 years. She enjoyed reading picture books to her students.

She has enjoyed the animals that have lived at her home over the years. Their antics and unique personalities have provided her with many stories to tell.

Her hobbies include birdwatching, nature walks, drawing, painting, and carving. She also enjoys entertaining children.

Eva desires to use her talents to the honor and glory of God. She is the author of *Blue Hen and Her Babies*, *Jasper's Secret*, *Little Pony*, *Heather the Sheep*, *Sam and His Friends*, and *Blackie the Crow*, also published by CAM. You can contact Eva by writing to her in care of Christian Aid Ministries, P. O. Box 360, Berlin, OH 44610.

About Christian Aid Ministries

Christian Aid Ministries was founded in 1981 as a nonprofit, tax-exempt 501(c)(3) organization. Its primary purpose is to provide a trustworthy and efficient channel for Amish, Mennonite, and other conservative Anabaptist groups and individuals to minister to physical and spiritual needs around the world. This is in response to the command to ". . . do good unto all men, especially unto them who are of the household of faith" (Galatians 6:10).

CAM supporters provide millions of pounds of food, clothing, Bibles, medicines, and other aid each year. Supporters' funds also help victims of disasters in the U.S. and abroad, put up Gospel billboards in the U.S., and provide Biblical teaching and self-help resources. CAM's main purposes for providing aid are to help and encourage God's people and bring the Gospel to a lost and dying world.